Joann Estoesta

## *About the Author*

GABRIEL SPERA'S poems have been published
in *Chicago Review, Crazyhorse, DoubleTake,
Epoch, Folio, The Greensboro Review, Laurel
Review, Michigan Quarterly Review, The
Missouri Review, New England Review,
Ontario Review, Poetry, Prairie Schooner,* and
*Southern Review.* His work also appears in
*The Best American Poetry 2000* and *The
Poetry Anthology, 1912–2002.* Spera grew up
in New Jersey, and was educated at
Cornell University and the University of
North Carolina, Greensboro. He lives in
Los Angeles.

# THE STANDING WAVE

The National Poetry Series was established in 1978 to ensure the publication of five poetry books annually through participating publishers. Publication is funded by the late James A. Michener, the Copernicus Society of America, Edward J. Piszek, the Lannan Foundation, the National Endowment for the Arts, and the Tiny Tiger Foundation.

2002 COMPETITION WINNERS
Julie Kane of Natchitoches, Louisiana, *Rhythm & Booze*
Chosen by Maxine Kumin, published by University of Illinois Press

William Keckler of Harrisburg, Pennsylvania, *Sanskrit of the Body*
Chosen by Mary Oliver, published by Viking Penguin

Eleni Sikelianos of Boulder, Colorado, *Footnotes to the Lambs*
Chosen by Diane Ward, published by Green Integer

Gabriel Spera of Los Angeles, California, *The Standing Wave*
Chosen by Dave Smith, published by HarperCollins

Meredith Stricker of Carmel, California, *Tenderness Shore*
Chosen by Fred Chappell, published by Louisiana State University Press

# THE STANDING WAVE

## POEMS

## GABRIEL SPERA

Perennial
*An Imprint of* HarperCollins*Publishers*

HarperCollins books may be purchased for educational, business, or sales promotional use. For information please write: Special Markets Department, HarperCollins Publishers Inc., 10 East 53rd Street, New York, NY 10022.

FIRST EDITION

*Designed by Nancy Singer Olaguera*

Library of Congress Cataloging-in-Publication Data

Spera, Gabriel
    The standing wave : poems / Gabriel Spera.—1st ed.
        p. cm.   (National poetry series)
    ISBN 0-06-054182-2
    I. Title. II. Series.

PS3619.P646S73 2003
811'.6—dc21

                                                                2002191936

02 03 04 05 06 ❖/RRD 10 9 8 7 6 5 4 3 2 1

# Acknowledgments

Some of these poems first appeared in other publications as listed below:

| | |
|---|---|
| *Chicago Review:* | "Beach Bum"; "Corcovado"; "Without a Sequel" |
| *Crazyhorse:* | "The Monarchs of El Rosario"; "Snake Farm" |
| *DoubleTake:* | "Idle Hands" |
| *Epoch:* | "José Mendías" |
| *Folio:* | "After the Peace" |
| *The Greensboro Review:* | "Traveler's Advisory" |
| *Laurel Review:* | "The Bats"; "Mosquito Spawn" |
| *Michigan Quarterly Review:* | "Leopard" |
| *The Missouri Review:* | "The Aerialist"; "Midway"; "Tarantula" |
| *New England Review/ Bread Loaf Quarterly:* | "The One That Almost Got Away" |
| *Ontario Review:* | "Vacation in Stone Harbor"; "Work Boots" |

*Poetry:*                 "Balkan"; "In a Field Outside the Town"; "My Ex-Husband"; "Sushi"

*Prairie Schooner:*      "All the Rage"; "Cleanliness"; "United Parcel"

*Southern Review:*      "The Mission Olive"; "Moon Jelly"

# Contents

# The Mission Olive

It's time, the day says, as it
always does, the coming rains
will rake them from the tree
if you don't first, the olives,
huge from months of purpling
like a hammerer's ripe thumb.
The lawn's peppered already
with the season's first windfall,
the flagstones bludgeoned where skins
have split open under feet
that track the ink indoors.
So I hobble, earth's butler,
up-ladder to the tree's great
relief, a plastic bucket
to receive the day's take.
My hand's small tongues grow blacker
in swallowing the dark fruit
dangling like gems of tar or
opulent mussels clustered
to some sea beast's restless
green and silvered mane. They thunk
into the pail like days
into a lifetime, bearing
down with the full heaviness
of their hidden gold of oil.

But though they've stuffed themselves
with sweet sun, still they taste
foul as bile—the faithless man
would surely chuck them. But
the patient man knows every
bitterness has its cure.
One fruit grower's handbook,
printed 1908, suggests
a broth of pot-ash lye, or
a months-long soaking in pure
well water, but the method
I favor's even older
than these words, passed down by a
people who knew how human
were the gods in all things, how
easy to manipulate.
Do nothing, they say, but leave
the new moons to wrinkle
in a colander, pomaced
in a mound of plain sea salt.
In two weeks' time, they'll forget,
as we all do, the source
of their hearts' pitched burning,
lose it in the harsh tears

their bodies will rain as they
soften into succulence,
helpless to resist the sweet
waking of their pearl-black flesh.

# Mosquito Spawn

Last week's rain has by now settled
and cleared in the wheelbarrow's kettle,
and the garden's grown hard enough to work.
And bowing to the handles,

I see them, ripening like questions
hung from my own reflection,
pimples forming in the water's skin,
rash-red and sickle-shaped, suggestions

of the measlers they'll become. And they panic
as I start to lift, the titanic
sloshing whipping them to frenzy.
They curl up like fingers, manic

with beckoning, mad for life. But my work
wants a wheelbarrow. So I jerk
the handles up and out they pour. No matter—
there's a city's worth welling in the murk

of lost pails and rumpled plastics fogged
with algae, plumping like the waterlogged
bodies of the drowned. In time, they'll burp free
from the water, take to the air, and dog

my dancing arms to exhaustion, guided
by breath trails and sworls of infrared,
embodying a hunger so perfect, so complete,
it can't even wait till I'm dead.

# The Bats

I cross the bridge, a walking
supper dish, a bowl of blood
that draws these shadows from the river,
swooping and crumpling through dusk.

They strafe my head, nibbling—
not my neck, but something near it—it's
the mayflies doubting round me
on wings the color of moon

across water, succulent truffles
of the air. How they give themselves
selflessly to myth, these caped
bugbears, brooding in attics and sultry

crevices by day, buckshotting forth
to cram their jowls with soul-white moths.
My skin goes milk and vinegar
at the merest thought of them,

denned in, groping and yammering
in the smother and flap, and yet,
glimpsed here, flashing like memory,
pure quick black against the dark,

in fact they flutter like the light
bounced into an overhang of leaves
above a koi pond, rapturous in their
breakfast acrobatics, further proof all

darkness ends in light, and the meekest
spirits will rise and sally out on the most
improbable of wings. If there is more
than hunger and striving and sex and sleep

I haven't known it, yet here
I am, in all wonder, the fleet brutes
squalling round me, moving visionless
in darkness, trusting, shouting as we go.

# Moon Jelly

A vitreous humor, pulsing in the nether, a living study
in the vagaries of joy. She is receptiveness
made flesh—or very nearly—the shallow bowl of her giving body
never filled. What does she care of up or down, of hour
or its opposite, what is the sea's wrath or hush
to her pliant design? She drifts in slow tumble with the flotsam
of sea-streams, her lambent arms conveying all that they caress
into translucence. Where in that frail form does she find the
    power
not to struggle, to renounce all ties to the jetty's fast stones?
Is she selfish to deny all thoughts of self, to wash
her hands of her own pale life, or is it simplest wisdom
to sink no teeth into the world, to leave no foot
or finger print, but to live as one already half gone,
a blooming sail, the merest scrim between here and not?

# José Mendías

I MET A TRAVELER FROM AN ANTIQUE LAND . . .

Riding nearly level to the train, the late-
day sun backlights the fortress of downtown,
teasing my eyes from a book, which, at this rate,
I'll never see the end of. And as the train rounds
a bend, an ambush of light suddenly scintillates
the graffiti, carved with a practiced hand
into the Plexiglas, the stroke bold and stark
as the calligraphy on an antique fan:
*José Mendías, 2 much 4 U,* a classic
example how the need to fix one's mark
to something pure and permanent as plastic
mars everything, reducing all we are to a dance
of light between two darknesses, a fantastic
hieroglyph, lost but for a brief translucence.

# Bliss

2:30 sharp, and they come tearing
like inmates out the high school doors,
furloughed again, heading towards
their cars lovingly shoehorned along the curb
of this normally spacious suburb,
ill equipped to see the irony of wearing

jeans they'll never grow into, skivvies
peeking above their belts to defy
an adult code that says what clothes to buy.
Their shorn heads unwittingly bounce
in time to the rap beats that announce
their arrival, a leitmotif so bass-heavy

it drives my windowpanes wild
with rattling. They've someplace better
to be, they'd have you know. Still, an hour later,
I swear I hear that same syncopated
headache. And I see why—there's an automated
radar machine set up down the road, brainchild

of some think-tank genius who surmised
we speed in ignorance, not bliss.
*Speed limit 35*, it says, *your speed is*
plastered in a huge bright digital chartreuse

that glares with disappointment. An effective ruse
for grown-up drivers who've internalized

their fear of discipline. Lacking such fear,
the kids haul past, pedal floored,
trying to peg the new high score,
then cruise round the block to start over.
Their yawping cuts through the mist of burnt rubber
and the heat from their engines melts the air.

# The Weaver's Error

Tripped by the motion of me, lugging sacks
of garbage to the bins, the driveway light
averts disaster, as I see her, starred
in the crabbed center of her galaxy
darned between the house eaves and the fence.
So wide a stitchwork seems beyond the scope
of one with neither memory nor foresight,
and yet I've caught her here before, rigging
this same contraption, linking point to point
without a blueprint or a diagram,
stealing upside down along her tightrope
or swinging her precarious trapeze.
Small wonder if it's something less than perfect
as men might reckon, the spokes off kilter, joints
all shy of plumb, each trapezoid a fall
from an ideal—unless of course each defect
is intended, is no flaw at all,
but subtly renders praise to something more,
for surely praise compels this work of grace,
this intricate mandala, more *te deum*
than tedium in its weave. Though hard to trace,
the supple swirl recalls the god's eyes
that the kids still make, the sunset-colored gems
of yarn spun round on wooden crosses, signs
that God sees all through lidless eyes. More gaze

than grab, the god of men—but her design
suggests a firmer power, more flesh than word,
judging by how she punctuates the air,
an asterisk, all tooth and eye, her bright
mercurial arms arrayed on trigger hairs.
She fills the core of her creation, focused,
radiantly displayed despite her tries
at self-effacement, her desire
to veil desire. Her world provides
what faith expects, rewards the trust
of sew and reap. She needn't sing
to draw the moths upon her shoals, they'll strand
themselves, in time, fixating on the void
she's framed in foam-bright filigree—or so
they would, if not for me, the monkey wrench,
foiling her machinations, revealing the wires
and sleights of several hands. But though exposed
for all she is, though looming like a bull's-eye
in the light, she holds her air of tense repose
as though her feast did not depend on my
not standing there, as though her world did more
than tolerate my sight. What isn't changed
for the worse each time I look at it, what perfection
would remain without my gaze? The better part
of all there is prefers that I not be—

yet here I am, inextricably stitched
in all I see, the flaw that shows the art.
And though my purpose may be hazy,
hers is clear. And so I duck her guylines, pitch
the trash, and close the kitchen door.
And sensing me no more, the driveway light
again lets fall the fabric of the night.

# Cleanliness

Kill the Buddha, Buddha said, annoyed
that no one took a word he uttered
literally. History doesn't record
how he washed his one saffron robe, but
most scholars agree he would've been
happier with a new Maytag with the
up-and-down supercleansing action and
low sudsing for fine washables. Clearly
the time it would've saved him, not having
to tramp down to the Ganges each week
to dunk his robe and hang around while it
sun dried, would've let him write
the poetry he always meant to, or at least
keep up with his correspondence.
In his most famous sermon, he didn't utter
a single word, and instead held up
a sole flower, perhaps representative
of the desire for springtime freshness
and whites as white as pure anemones.
Seven years he sat in a dank cave
groping toward enlightenment about the wheel
of time, the cycle of renewal, the soul
colorfully tumbling and jostling
through the world until it grows so soiled
with life, the threads go bare in a flash

of untailorable nirvana. A sleek
front-loader might've saved him years
of shivering, and freed him up to spend
more time with the kids—the neighbors' kids,
the ones with the grass stains on their knees
flashing like eternity.

# Traveler's Advisory

Notice things—
a mast like a metronome, ticking;

the local trollers reeling in fishlines
tugged by clinging sea stars and brangle,

and casting back to the silty brine
where urchins search anchors on the sea floor;

beached skiffs along the shore;
darned webs of fishnet

set soaking in the toweling sun
or else heaped in bushel baskets

like thin spaghetti, or squid;
gates made of lashed branches, latched yet

not locked, spanning gaps in low stone walls
enfolding groves of olive and fig;

high hills like a throw rug's bunched lumps
lumbering up from the sea plain;

forgotten cottages strewn with the sorry spall
of red tile and alabaster, succumbing

to slow encroachment from clumps
of tanned grasses, dead tree husks;

lugsails at dock, lulled in tidal flux.
Note how contentment comes,

not vague and ebbed like plump
jellyfish, but grips quick as a lizard

skitting through rocks, or the bird
who swoops to pick him off.

## Beach Bum

I catch him as he kicks his sneakers off
and crabs his arms back, grabbing at his shirt,
backs out of it and drops it in a heap,
undoes his fly and shimmies off his pants,
thumbs the loose elastic of his shorts
around his ankles and just tiptoes out
into the water, spritzing ribs and arms,
his hairy shanks and belly, squatting down
and bobbing back, pincing his nose to plunk
at last full under, scrunching fingers through
his scalp, surfacing in a drape of foam
and knuckling clear the salt sting from his eyes.
He turns and, paddling, skates back through the swells
to shore and waits there, his eyes half open, fingers meshed
behind his head, the small, forgotten penis
drying saltly in the languid air
as though the slick of bodies sprawled about
on towels, drowsing in the rising haze,
weren't there, or were blind, or were each one
lost in someone else's dirty world.

# The One That Almost Got Away

Too young to realize how the odds
are stacked, he winds up like a discus thrower
and, whirling, casts the shining hook
his father's hidden in a bean-size wad

of bread. It arcs away from him and plinks
into the sea, the excess thread
scribbling the water's bilgy surface
before it, too, inch by inch, sinks.

A school of yellow sunfish shies
like thieves up to the bait. Flashing,
they dash and peck until one gulps it whole
and gets nipped neatly up, its eyes

wide as the fisher's father, who
shrugs and winnows out the hook. The wet fish
wriggles free from his slick fingers,
and slapping the hard dock flaps back into

its shallow element. It shimmies, tilts,
but sinks among the algaed junk,
coaxing a mottled brooder from some jug's
black cave, oozing out through silt

plumes. Cloudily gliding, it storms
over the bottomed wrack like a rumor, tangled
in thickets of its own wrangling,
to trap the fish in a confusion of arms.

Pointing at this sea monster, the boy
tugs his father's shirtsleeve, but he
is not the hero that he used to be,
and has no power to save what want destroys.

# Corcovado

Parable of balance, proving false the
laws that ground us, Christ's statue hovers
like a diver
transfixed mid-swan and gliding like balsa
crisp in the stalled wind. Seen from afar,
his form, like a cast of glazed porcelain,
shines clean
and seamless, perfect, whole and small. It's only here
beneath the toes of his great blocked feet
that cracks in his marbly robes appear, embossed
with the black moss
that spreads like night across the slick concrete,
while far below, the ferries hoot, the gangplanks swarm,
the sidewalks speckle, and like a crinkled ball
of cellophane, all
the waking world dartles beneath his calling arms.
Surely this is how it was, the Temptation—
Christ set aloft on a sky-crowned pedestal,
those cities sprawled
before him, growing clear, nearing as his vision
stretched to comprehend every scrabbled
inch of brilliance, skewed as in a globed mirror
with the power
of holding all, and in an instant. The ripples

forming off the ocean's distant ridge
would live for seeming days before toppling like rows
of beaching dominoes,
or bending round the bay cape where the causeway bridge
bounds across the water like the path of a skipped stone.
And he would be lured, surely, by the trucks
plowing like mollusks
down the glistering freeways, the half-crown
of islands that pacify the harbor, where yawls
anchored off the yacht club docks, like minnows
browsing, nose
the coming currents with their sleek bright hulls
all schooled and aligned. How could anyone trade
all this—these buildings, vying like pine, nestled
in the mountain's muscle,
the valley rifts filled with the jumbled cascade
of white-walled houses, ruby roof tiles,
the tiny crowd gathered for the trundling bus
and cabs that rush
and pause along the cemetery's griddled miles . . .
It can only be that from that height,
where even the high-rise hotels along the strand
seem to stand
no taller than stacked fruit crates—from there, no naked eye

could spot the box town beneath the road bridge,
the young curled up on sewer grates,
or the men who scrape
mussels from foul rocks in the bay sludge
to roast in coffee tins, or else there would've been
more wavering, more rage, for wouldn't peace on earth
best be served
on earth? With such rich splendors tagged in heaven,
wouldn't staying bring the purer sacrifice?
He could only have been blinded to the several hells
of living, or else
he'd never believe just one death could suffice,
would've stayed to embrace the world more completely,
would've left us more than just a thin, pale shadow
inching slow
across a vast city, cast obliquely
from the peak of this fathomless height,
a mendicant redeemer who reascends into the sky
when daylight dies
abandoning all the world to the mercy of night.

# City of Refuge, Kona Coast

A late-day breeze wrests
from the palms a hush
like sugar leaking
from a sack, and mangoes
soften in a peppering
of fruit flies. Hard to believe
here in any laws, barring
the obvious, but for
the man who broke them, given
but a slim head start,
these walls and fishponds,
windbreaks and huts held
out the one hope for
redemption. It's home
to turtles now, breaking
with their beaks the lagoon's
reflection of the
every-colored day, blinking
like sleepwalkers roused
by the hollow sound of
their own held breath at last
let go. Off-limits
to the tin packers and
comb makers, they drift
untroubled through clear

shallows, wheeling like
dirigibles, working
the soft oars of their
arms in calm strokes, as though
time, like light, bent beneath
the surface, as though their
bodies were no slaves
to the empire of air.
Two tiki, fearsome
in their humanity, snarl
from the canoe launch,
warding off now only
errant snorkelers and
picture takers while crabs
the color of papayas
click their limbs like knives
and forks across pillows
of stone and the turtles,
jaded with sea leaves,
sea-logged, lug the swamped
boats of their bodies
upon the rocks, stretching
their necks as though dragged
by an unseen fishline.
Humped like spent volcanoes,

THE STANDING WAVE

they nod off, lulled by the surf
of their own breathing, safe
from the water's hunger,
but ready to slip
like coins into the lapping,
sinking glimmeringly
from hand to memory.

## Snake Farm

God knows how they got good at this,
the small men in safari suits chasing
long noodles and fish balls with American
cigarettes, plodding like postmen
to terrariums crammed with ficus leaves
limed with fresh scat. They seem to think death
couldn't be bothered with the world's
inexhaustible poor, by the way they snake
arms through lids and trapdoors, dropping
white mice with no great urgency, no
reverence for the small gods turbaned
in the branches, more beautiful than evil
need be—the pit viper, cream-lipped vine
of kiwi green, the banded krait,
a yellow pepper charred by fire, the mangrove,
beetle-black and ringed with false golds—
all command the same indifference, the men
ignore them like the cameras clicking
in their ears, bored with the world
of hand biters, too familiar with the daily threat
of pain. They know the greatest power
strikes least. Even the cobra pit
they stroll through like a hen yard,
disturbing the clay pots where they drowse,
gaffing them out into a gunnysack to spill

before the tourists, sweaty, hungry
for the exotic after days of common poverty,
tantalized by this richness, this king
moving like a runnel off a dirt road
in the rain. And when it slides too close
to their backpedaling feet, the handlers haul it
by the whip end of its tail back until
it rears up, a tension, an imminent
reprisal, head held level above the neck's nearly
sensual undulations. It is the snake that charms,
lulls, what it kills—a trick it falls for,
fixing on a left hand while a right
slaps from behind. And as though there were
doubts about the stakes, as though
to prove some higher purpose, they wedge
a saucer in its grin and press a pearl
of venom out, extending it to the rattled crowd
who see in this slick glycerin only
the promise of a thirsty death and not
the chance to make a small life on bare feet.

# The Monarchs of El Rosario

Backdrop to our trudging, the purling of their wings
rings through the sagging boughs of pine they leave
deciduously drifting groundward, ambering

all they light on. Stand where the sunlight cleaves
the busy air, and they touch down on legs long
as eyelashes, batting the fine down of bared sleeves,

tickling like a stomachful of nerves. Their tongues
curl like burners on electric stoves, sheened
with weed milk, wings like shutters flung

open to the wide day, cayenne-colored, veined
with char. Even the unflappable peasants,
glutting the small market for silk-screened

T-shirts, hair clips, pencils, and pendants
stand simple with awe to see them baubling the air
like something they should know better than want.

And yet, for them, migration's nothing rare,
or being born into a life already dispossessed
of all but a sense of origin. Instinctively, their

children cup the fallen too caked with the dust
cattled up by an unsustainable wealth
of tourists and blow them clean with a quick gust

of breath. And when they set them back upon the shelf
of air, they watch them go as though remembering
when gold was for giving, and the sun itself
descended on wings of flame to walk with kings.

# Tarantula

The boys are taunting it with a leg-long stick—
diverting it from whatever purpose
compels this living scribble across the weathered planks
stacked along the shed. The color of burlap
and coffee grounds, a fat knot, a greedy hand,
it somehow glides—when not stopped—
with the grace of a harvester
roiling above the fields. Not nearly as deadly
as they dream, still it pricks
their imaginations, this creeper through corncribs,
this crawler up walls, reclusive spindler
with powers that defy its flyweight size.
And they can squash it with a good stomp or stone
but so far haven't, held in check
by something closer to reverence
than mere mischief, something quickened
by the sight of what can kill
without remorse or retribution.
It is an arsenal, an acid—even
they must hold their distance, though they
hunger for its risk of sudden fury, for its being
beyond the reach of human hands.
They want control, they want destruction
on demand, want something punished
for no good reason, they want this tangler

to react to their tapping stick, to swarm,
like need, all arms and eyes, over something
pitiful and small, but all it does is freeze—
and not in fear but calculation, unwilling
to surrender the least pinch of its reserve.
And so they lean in, grinning as though
trying a father's patience, or as though
they'd gained some mastery of this killer
that shows no inkling, no concern,
that its every moment hangs by the filament
of their whim. They are not humbled
by the flawless machinery of its form,
they have not learned yet to judge power
by restraint—and still they fling their crooked stick
to the far weeds and crouch in silence as it
sidles back to the dark that gave it shape.

# Vacation in Stone Harbor

Even the locals like it here, and you
have come to feel at home, too, listening as
the honks of outbound charter boats punch through
the whine of iron cabling ratcheting
the bridge the causeway ends in, as you queue

to cross the channel, raking nits of sand
already from your scalp. From next door's roof
drifts down the clacks of shingling hammers, and
a tinny radio's outdated tunes.
The hardware store can't stock too many cans

of beige paint, and the realtor's window front's
collaged with this year's crop. The barkeep says
he grinds the horseradish himself, and sets
beside your mug a snifter cockled with
crisp oyster crackers. In summer months

a stand just off the sand road's shoulder sells
real key lime pie, grilled corn, and fresh-shucked clams.
Out back's a dock. The water splunks the piles,
where shards of crabs in crab traps bluster, wedged
with chicken necks beneath their barbarous gills.

Even the kids haul cratefuls, and spin tales
of oysters hunkered in the mudflats grown
to rowboat size. Tanned anglers leave their reels
and tackle idle while they grab a bite,
the day's catch swishing deep in plastic pails.

Even when you're not home, you find you leave
the house unlocked, the bikes out front, and when
old men wheel shopping carts along the street
don't even look away, because you know they're filled
with groceries, of course, just groceries.

# My Ex-Husband

That's my ex-husband pictured on the shelf,
Smiling as if in love. I took it myself
With his Leica, and stuck it in that frame
We got for our wedding. Kind of a shame
To waste it on him, but what could I do?
(Since I haven't got a photograph of you.)
I know what's on your mind—you want to know
Whatever could have made me let him go—
He seems like any woman's perfect catch,
What with his ruddy cheeks, the neat mustache,
Those close-set, piercing eyes, that tilted grin.
But snapshots don't show what's beneath the skin!
Sure, he'd a certain charm, charisma, style,
That passionate, earnest glance he struck, meanwhile
Whispering the sweetest things, like, "Your lips
Are like plump rubies, eyes like diamond chips,"
Could flush the throat of any woman, not
Just mine. He knew the most romantic spots
In town, where waiters, who all knew his face,
Reserved an intimately dim-lit place
Half hidden in a corner nook. Such stuff
Was all too well rehearsed, I soon enough
Found out. He had an attitude—how should
I put it—smooth, self-satisfied, too good
For the rest of the world, too easily

Impressed with his officious self. And he
Flirted—fine! but flirted somehow a bit
Too ardently, too blatantly, as if,
If someone ever noticed, no one cared
How slobbishly he carried on affairs.
Who'd lower herself to put up with shit
Like that? Even if you'd the patience—which
I have not—to go and see some counselor
And say, "My life's a living hell," or
"Everything he does disgusts, the lout!"—
And even if you'd somehow worked things out,
Took a long trip together, made amends,
Let things get back to normal, even then
You'd still be on the short end of the stick;
And I choose never, ever to get stuck.
Oh, no doubt, it always made my limbs go
Woozy when he kissed me, but what bimbo
In the steno pool went without the same
Such kisses? So, I made some calls, filed some claims,
All kisses stopped together. There he grins,
Almost lovable. Shall we go? I'm in
The mood for Chez Pierre's, perhaps, tonight,
Though anything you'd like would be all right
As well, of course, though I'd prefer not to go
To any place with checkered tables. No,

We'll take my car. By the way, have I shown
You yet these lovely champagne flutes, hand-blown,
Imported from Murano, Italy,
Which Claus got in the settlement for me!

## United Parcel

At his console, the foreman shunted boxes
without mercy, by the clock, until they
buckled like a train wreck at the spit end
of the chute. Who'd expect kindness
for the packages marked "Fragile," plucked
from that trembling logjam? If not
stepped on or punted outright, they'd sail
the truck's length like put shots, arcing over
the fat boxes already rising like debt
in the triple-digit heat. Above the shush
and whump of parcels dropping onto belts,
the air ducts hiving, the diesel farting,
the loudspeaker radio churned out
heavy metal. In the bay one over, Andy—
God knows how he survived, dropping
half his doughy weight in the sweat
that dragged his T-shirt to his knees—
Andy sang to his favorite tune, played
three times a shift, the music itself
an automation, thunking, whining, insisting
*we're not gonna take it, no, we're not*
*gonna take it, we're not gonna take it*
*anymore.* Clearly he gave no thought
to the lyrics, which all the same freed him
from his body's soulless mechanics.

Me, I hated that song, hated the inane
refrain, the hot-rod beat, hated Andy's
head-jerking bliss at feeling finally
understood—what didn't I hate then, humping
my back, pitching boxes into greedy
gaping trucks, ragging my hands
with my own salt and cardboard dust, what
joy could I take knowing whatever
it was, however he shouted otherwise
in a song he didn't write but felt he could've,
Andy would take it—we all would, for the rest
of our parceled lives. *Come on, feel
the noise*, the song urged. And we did.

## Work Boots

Put yourself in my shoes, he says,
thirteen years at the plant to the point
where you go to work and you read
the paper, and even the shift
you run could be halved,
the men just pushing buttons while parts
pick by on gantryways, bound
for plating in thick
baths of nickel and chrome.
Think about all the identical hours
you've clocked since the days
when you first hired on, since the days
when you used to come early for work,
so long ago now,
you can't even picture what car
you were driving, what a
sandwich cost. And sure, you'd do more,
run the whole damn rig by yourself,
but even then, say there was
more work and no union, say the
factory was newer, say anyone gave
two shits for this town,
there's still nothing can keep
them from packing up shop
for Mexico, likely, and think

about having to start
all over, with nothing, and at
your age, back on some cramped
assembly line, soldering piece
after piece, potting, staking, your hands
by the end of the shift
too tired even to crunch
the stiff pale card that the clock
whittles down each day like a bone,
the pneumatic press the fiend in your dreams,
the song you can't drink out of your head
when you meet at the regular bar
all the regular faces, amazed
like raccoons from the stamp
of safety goggles, the scent
of solvent clinging like wax
in their hair, while their jaws
hang slacker with each
cheap glass, until they stagger outside
to a train of taxis who know
without telling where's home.
Put myself in his shoes, he says,
as though his life were boots to be kicked
off, boots any man could just slip
on, lace up, and move through his days,

with no one the wiser, and no
questions asked, and nobody to
turn to and say, no, listen, you don't
understand, this isn't my life.

# Idle Hands

We're shoveling the sheetrock, bricks, and planks
the builders couldn't use into a pocked
and rusted pickup, settling in the clay
outside the condos springing up around
what will be cul-de-sacs, when all at once
we see this snake come trickling through the gutter
licking slackly over tire treads sunk
from lumbering machines, and one of our
small crew, career odd-jobber, Keith, jumps up,
runs over, plants his steel-toed shoes, and hoists
his shovel, set to hack its head clean off—
but not yet, not before he watches it
recoil from where his shadow falls, almost
not smiling his first smile all day, and from
somebody else's mouth it seems I hear
my voice say, "Wait, it's just a garter snake,
it's harmless, just forget it, let it go."
And so he turns to me, his face the face
of someone stopped from beating something
he clearly feels he owns, he turns and says,
" 'S that so? Well now, if you're so fucking sure,
go pick it up. Go 'head, right now." I can't
begin to guess how many snakes I held
when I was younger, treadmilling my hands
beneath their waterfalling bodies, but

enough. Time was, I'd prowl through sagging barns
looking for them, and knew the bleached flat stones
where they'd be scrawled out, knew exactly where
to grab them to keep that trap of fishhook teeth
from clamping on my thumb, yet now I can't
be sure of anything, except how bad
Keith wants it dead, and not because he thinks
it's poisonous. Snakes I know, but hate
like Keith's is hard to figure. So I keep
my peace until he jabs, "Time's up," and watch
him work his shovel like a butter churn,
catching, scritching, shredding the luckless thing
in bows and ribbons into dirt.

# All the Rage

Only psychos and felons got tattoos back then,
which covered everyone I worked with on the truck—
Fitch, who lost a rose-twined dagger with half the skin
on both legs when his bike jumped a median, struck
a streetlamp, and combusted. Or Pete, with the mermaid
he still showed off like a new bride, trying in vain
to make it shimmy on his arm, blind to the grayed
green tail and blur of what years back had been a smile.
Even Blatz, with his army-navy drabs, wound
a thread around a needle tip, dipped it in a vial
of India ink, and pecked out across the fat mound
of his thumb a skewed gunmetal-green-black
swastika. That should've been enough. And yet I found
myself strangely tempted, watching Donny with his slack
side-eyed saunter climb the loading dock,
indifferent to the diesel and seven-o'clock cold,
setting his coffee on the punch clock, a hard-pack rolled
in his shirt's short sleeves, baring the rocks
of his biceps, lit up like a beachside casino
in blues and vermilions, bright forms that stole
from his knuckles to elbows, elbows
to collarbone. And while the rest of us, blessed
with nothing to hold out for anyway, cashed
our paychecks at the pool hall Friday nights, he stashed
what he could of his away, saving up, obsessed,

evidently, with gemming over the arms he'd once
used to beat a decent man to near death
in a life-staining minute that bought him nine months
in Riverfront. And we few of no design, who knew less
beauty than truth, who would always equate
violence with strength, could not help appreciate
how the foreman gave him space. How suddenly foolish
I felt, when I asked him, one such morning
he showed up, skin swollen beneath a jewelish
sheen of baby oil, some new tensed beast adorning
his already busy forearms, when I asked, because
I could picture him with his fist flopped
like a blood donor's on a vinyl tabletop,
the walls papered with available designs, the buzz
like a streetlamp on the fritz, when I asked in
all innocence if it hurt, having that needle pop
again and again and again the drum of his skin.

# Kindness

It's the small acts of kindness I take strength in, acts
of grace so beautiful and true, they make me weep
with reckless hope. Just take this story of the five
who went out cruising in the canyons after dark
and found a car parked on an empty stretch of road.
They smashed the windshield, slashed the tires, jammed
    the locks,
and drove away—but then turned back to see if there
were anything inside the car worth taking. It's then
they find the owners, two young couples, early teens
who'd sneaked away from home to watch the stars come out
and kiss. They rush them, beat the boys, and drag the girls
into the brush. The one, her skirt half torn away,
pinned down, looks up and begs the stranger straddling her,
don't kill me, please, don't kill me. Shut your mouth, he says,
don't look me in the face, you'll be all right, and moves
a hand down to his belt. She turns her head, and says
as though to no one in the world, then kiss my cheek,
as a promise you won't kill me when it's done. And so
he pauses, perched above her, silent, though the dark
is queasy with the sound of muffled sobs, he stops
and kisses her wet cheek, and I, who've judged my kind
most harshly always, I with no good word for men,
can only hang my head to know the emptiness,
the pity, in this small and stunning act of grace.

# Sushi

Pared to a near essence, a mere
intention, his motions
flow with the offhanded grace
of mating jellyfish, arms oddly beefy,
smooth as anything loved too much
by the sea. Fingers chilled
to a pale rice color, he eases
a moon-streak of knife through thick flesh
clean as the shark's fin splitting the air,
untouched by hesitation, shaving
rich steaks with more consistency
than a calm lake slaps its shore.
Each spoonful of uni, heaped
upon a finger-width of rice,
luminous moons atop a backdrop
of black lacquer, begs the question
what nourishes more, fish
or artifice, consumption
or consummation of a flesh both
raw and fully prepared, perfected
by the mastery of his hands made
vassal to our hunger? Reminiscent
of nothing that teems and multiplies,
the tongues of ahi nonetheless speak
to something in our sea-swollen vessels

still tugged at by the sea and something
in our souls with no taste
for the bodily, oddly embarrassed
by the need, the act, of eating.
Inscrutable in squid-white apron, he
leads us, lures us, to the source,
presents something so nearly still
swimming, we can all but taste
its last sensations, its final desire:
not to die, not for us, not to finish
its life of feast and fleeing sliced
upon the cutting board of time to serve
something like a god, but more
sensual, more ravenous, more
likely to want more than we are.

# Leopard

First warm Saturday of spring, and the city pier
is a hazard of whizzing hooks and lines, a hatchery
of white ten-gallon paint tubs aslosh with the rare
unlucky smelt. No one seems to mind the radio

drowning out the gulp of oily water hitting
the tarred piles, or the pit bull snoozing in the shade
of a trash can, indifferent to the signs forbidding
dogs, kites, liquor, and skateboards. It is the sort

of day folks from out of town wish will never
ever end, and even the kids in from the east side, brave
or hungry enough to eat what this water offers,
seem to envy no one, and have all they could want. At once

a long rod doubles over, a sudden question, an alarm
that sends a man in tank top reeling along the rail,
under and behind the other fishlines, his thick arms,
lettered in a gothic font, leveraging the butt

of his pole against his thickly buckled belt. "Leopard,"
he calls, the one flat word a signal or command
that brings two friends or brothers with a lanyard
and grappling hook. They uncoil the yellow rope

like cops cordoning a crime scene, peering over the railing,
saying, "Hold on to 'im, just a minute, almost there . . ."
And suddenly hands are waving, voices calling,
bodies bending to the sea like queasy passengers

to see it—a three-footer, maybe, its back the bamboo-
green of sunlight spearing just beneath the surface
of a lagoon, moving as though its blunt head knew
nothing of the hook sunk in its jaw. And truly,

it is beautiful, and its swerves and angles slice
the small waves with the ease of God's own finger,
its body slaloming, sleek, untainted by malice
or doubt, unafraid of anything that moves beneath its sky,

so perfect, even the man who's snagged it all but neglects
to notice how the whole dock surrounds him, so intent
he is on snaring his prize, he hardly sees he connects
the whole crowd like a common belief or enemy,

brings them together, shoulder to shoulder, to watch the trinity
of hooks descend, to watch the youngest brother swing,
jerk, and set one hook between the winged symmetry
of its fins and the lash of tail. And as they start

hoisting it, fist by fist, up thirty feet of clear drop,
no one backs away, no one, it seems, even considers
what they'll do once this single-minded hunger is plopped
dead in their midst, too big for buckets, a violence

made flesh, no one wonders why they didn't cut bait
to begin with, why anyone would want to see such power
unmade. But they never do—confused by its new weight
in the air, the shark thrashes, slaps, rolls as though frenzied

with feeding, ripping its thick skin from the hook,
snapping the fishline in its gums with an unexpected
flash of foam-blue stomach, deceptively soft, the crook
of its mouth like a reaper's scythe, all teeth and no tongue.

It shimmies off, with bait in gullet, as the man in tank top reels
his weightless catch of air back to the pier. And the crowd,
no longer of one mind, no longer selfless, uncongeals,
still picturing the small and fleeting beauty they would not spare.

# Balkan

As if it were crisp onion skin
that might flake free, with every step
the stretcher bearers took, the char
that patched her grizzled arms curled back,
and knucklebones broke through the snarl
of fingers shriveled into claws,
while from one nakedly dangling limb,
scraping the blacktop, dark drops fell.
And as the awkward litter drew
within the scope of the camera's lens,
because he couldn't bear his half
one-handed, one hand on her head,
nor fully block it with his sleeve,
the man who held the torso end
could not obscure the gaping chock
that the slit that crossed her neck became
each time the jostled head lolled back
as if on hinges. Throat thrown wide,
and vented like an organ pipe,
it seemed, if only lungs would gorge
and bellow, she still might sound a keen
so true that the world must break against it.

# In a Field Outside the Town

Three days later, Suljic was finally given a drink
of water and marched with a dozen other men
onto a small livery truck, one of two, fenced
along each side by wooden planks,

the back left open to give a clear shot
to the automatic weapon poking out the window
of the red sedan that followed, the squat nose
trained on them, ridiculously, as if they'd any thought

of hopping off a moving truck. Suljic peered
vacantly through the slats. He'd missed the yellow flowers
of spring and by now saw a landscape taken over
by summer, the grasses closing behind them as they veered

from the road and lurched across cow paths. They drove
to the center of a wide field and stopped. Old sweat,
without the breeze of movement, prickled in the heat.
A metal smell drifted, an untended apple grove

baked on a hill, and the weeds droned, motory with bees.
But Suljic noticed none of these, fixed instead
on the gaps in the field where bodies, all dead,
matted down the wild carrot and chicory, their khakis

splotched darkly, like a fawn's dappled haunches
obscuring them. The men clambered down into the tall grass
and lined up at gunpoint. Suljic was sure the last
good thing he'd ever see would be the apple branches

drooping with fruit, but the man beside him grabbed
his hand, and looked him in the face, as if
Suljic, just a bricklayer, had any assurances to give.
He squeezed the hand back, hard, and felt a scab

crossing the man's knuckles. He saw, too, a thin scar
worrying the arch of his left eyebrow, much older,
perhaps from a fall as a child from a ladder
picking fruit. His hand was like a clump of mortar,

and three nights without sleep had webbed his eyes red.
And Suljic suddenly stuttered to ask his name,
what town was he from, his job—anything—but there came
the crackle, like sometimes thunder, undecided

whether to begin, that starts, stalls, then trips
over itself, the sound crinkling from one
end of the sky to the other. The sound took possession
of his face until it, too, crinkled, his grip

pulsed, and he fell forward. Suljic winced
in the tackle of bodies, and splayed down in the dirt
flattening himself like a beetle, not hurt
in any new way, not yet convinced

he wasn't dead and didn't feel it. He heard the click
of fresh clips sliding into place, and shut
his eyes lightly, sure someone had seen he wasn't shot
and would come finish it. But no one came. Another truck

rolled up. The men climbed down, and lined up, docilely.
He recognized, solely by rhythm, a prayer, cut off
by the crackle, the hush of crickets, the soft
whump of bodies folding at the knees

and knocked by bullets shoulder first
into the grass. No one yelled. No one tried to run.
Another truck, another group, falling like a succession
of bricks sliding off a hod. Suljic finally pissed

where he lay, and blended in all the better
with the others. The noise stopped, and he cracked
his eyes enough to see, across the backs
like bleeding hills, a man strolling along the scatter

of bodies with a pistol, putting a slug
into the skull of anyone that still twitched
or mumbled. Then came the snort and low-pitched
rumble of diesel engines as two backhoes dug

a trench along the margin of all the collapsed
bodies. Impossibly, the crackling started anew,
and when darkness finally settled, the squads continued
in what light the backhoes' headlights threw. Perhaps

the shooting was over long before the sound
left him, the crackle to his eardrums
was like the rolling of a boat to his limbs
echoing long after he'd reached dry ground.

The soldiers left. Still he didn't move, but eased
his eyes full open. The moon above the orchard
was shrinking higher, its light glossing the awkward
pale forms that stubbled the dry weeds,

glinting off teeth and eyes. He scuttled from beneath
the arms and legs flopped sleepingly over
his own, as though by drunkards or lovers,
and rose like a foal to his numb feet,

seeing throughout the field no man not touched
by three dead others. He stood for a moment, trying
to guess, even roughly, their number, multiplying
bodies per square meter, but the math was too much,

the count too huge. He stared at the faces beside him
in the grass, like a man leaving something he knew
he would someday have to return to,
looking for the landmarks that would guide him—

the crooked teeth, the welted cheek, the pale eyes eclipsed
by half-shut lids, lolling upward, inward, swollen
as though with weeping, blood from an unseen hole
glistering down a chin line, crusting on lips.

How could he explain his life, what could he say
to those who weren't here to see, to the mothers and wives
who'd swear for years their men were still alive,
somewhere, the bodies never found, bulldozed into clay—

would he tell them how he tiptoed, unable to avoid
stepping on hands and ankles, or how the tears
like a secret he'd harbored through three years
of siege shook loose, and how he let them, no longer afraid

of being found out and cut down by gunfire,
or how he ran anyway, when he reached the open, quick
as his bum leg would let him, without a look
back at the faces turned like gourds in the dark mire.

# After the Peace

Even the clean ones, plowed up on a trowel,
the peat clopped off, the fabric stripped away,
don't glare so starkly as the cotton masks
cocooned across the faces of the men
who dredge the soil with tongs and plastic bags,
unearthing piece by piece a pebbled knee,
a bolt of shin, a hip, a fence of ribs.
They lift their heads like cattle, briefly, as
another jeep pulls up. Two men get out
and cross the field, with clipboards, jotting notes
and nudging bones. One dips a glove to cup
a dark skull not quite shucked of hair, and worms
a finger through the hole shocked in its base.
He globes it round to show the exit starred
into the cheekbone like a socket or
a tongue-full cavity, as though two eyes
were not enough to see with, one mouth one
too few to speak what happened this time here.
He lobs it back, slaps clean his palms, and slings
his camera out. It is enough for most
to guess such fields exist, but far away
are men who do not trust in words, but must
have pictures they can hold up to the light.

# The Suicide Bombers

They have never thrown stones across the settled mirror of an
alpine pond breathing in the pine-suffused mist of rising
evening.

They have never been disarmed by the incongruous ballet of
slag-dark suits and pendular briefcases surging and bobbing
through crosswalks past the still-cool cars bumper-locked
outside offices of chiseled stone and implacable skyrise glass.

They have never seen a school of circus-colored reef fish
startled and dervishing with one mind through the speckled
coral and lava floes bedding the shoals of a dead volcano.

They have never known peace.

They have never been ambushed by the thick pervasion of
honeysuckle overwhelming the fence behind the Little
League dugout.

They have never stripped naked and slipped into a snow-lodge
Jacuzzi beneath a million pinprick stars swabbing their
foreheads with bottles of chilled pale ale.

They have never launched a flatboat through the agonized
twists of bearded trees rising from a greened-over swamp
rife with the buzz and sputter of winged bugs and the sump-
pump groan of bullfrogs.

They have never trusted words.

They have never risen up atop a bald basalt dome and spread
their arms and legs to catch the sage-scented air thermaling

up from a valley unearthly with the sparse forbidding stands of ocotillo and blade-limbed Joshua tree.

They have never strewn their weary limbs beside pup tents pitched on a tundra of flat gray stones beside a glacier watching the Northern Lights spill like powdered sugar through the sky.

They have never set a fire of grayed wood on a night of road-erasing snow and rumpled down into a worn leather armchair to watch *Casablanca* for the umpteenth time.

They have never lost God.

They have never obtained a state of mindful nothingness driving and driving through the time-shredding always of a young field of fountainous corn stampeded by the hayriding winds of early summer.

They have never been blessed with a flawless martini on the porch of a weather-bleached Cape Codder overlooking the reedy-grassed dunes counting the seconds between the blue flash and thunderous booming clamoring out to sea.

They have never sought refuge from a sunshower beneath the faded red-and-white awning of a fruit stand giddy in the warm drizzle-scent evanescing from the roadtop like a historied perfume.

They have never wept with joy.

# The Aerialist

(PHILIPPE PETIT, AUGUST 7, 1974, NEW YORK)

Here goes nothing, he thinks, taking his first small resolute step, here goes nothing. Through the soles of his tight shoes, the iron wire goes effortlessly to the crease in the balls of his feet, as he starts, effortlessly, walking as if on air, his posture stiff as a young debutante's walking holding books on her head. The long slight frown of pole he's holding amplifies every least muscle tremor, each pause, shift, regroup, amplifies how little room there is for error, how much hangs in the balance, how most men could never follow. The straightest path is always the most difficult to stick to—everyone knows that—though what's most difficult points us most directly to heaven. The taut cable, from all viewpoints but his, cuts the world neatly in half, a bold slice, a dividing line, but he doesn't buy those outdated dualities, left and right, east and west, he refuses to choose, refuses to swerve, insists there's another way, refuses even to lean. He's reached an accord between two ends that are even after all. How high is he? A hundred stories? As if that mattered—after so many floors, the stakes are the same. But as for the crowd, so many hundreds of feet below, they have no real idea. There must be hundreds, complete strangers, gathered like brothers, bound by their complete wonder and tension. Do they want him to succeed, he can't help wonder, hoping to take part in his literal transcendence? Or are they all hoping secretly he'll fail, so they can go back to their pedestrian lives, secretly convinced that none fall farther and harder than those who've convinced themselves they're above it all? Maybe both. Or neither. They themselves surely don't know, and he doesn't need to take sides. Not now, surely.

At last the edge of Tower Two appears a few feet away, and he's at last aware of the crowd, police, photographers, helicopters. He's not aware how long it took to get this far—minutes? days? hours?—or how long until it's all over. Hold steady now, he thinks, the prize is never lost until practically in hand. Everyone knows that. Take it easy—you've practically assured your place in history—the city won't forget. You can rest assured. This is your moment, not the next. What's next? Fill your lungs with this rarest of air, slightly redolent of the river, fill your eyes with this rarest picture of downtown, hear the clicks of cameras snapping endless pictures, force your arms to bear up a little longer. Savor this instant, which no force on earth can take away. Soon, you'll be firmly, humanly, back on earth—there's no getting around it, no looking back. One step, and you're there.

## Eyelash

A black slash, a brushstroke, sleek
bristle, sharp thistle of the eye's scant lid—
who hasn't wished on one
astray, or brushed its grin from love's flushed cheek?
Who hasn't shed his share
of tears to find the eye undone
by what it took for granted,
blind to what had always stood most near?

# Midway

The same arcs repeat themselves everywhere
my eye goes—the same measured
progression, same illusion of narrative.
Take now: I am cranking one end
of a jump rope tethered to a fence
of my own making while my daughter
skips, singing a song with no meaning,
no purpose outside the simple repetition
of sound. And as it rises and curls,
falls and scoops, the rope traces through the air
a helix too subtle to be perceived—
I see only a circle radiating
from my wrist, she sees a simple
repetition of lines like the frames
of a broken film reel, or the crossbars
of a Ferris wheel. She gravitates naturally
to the midpoint, where time
and space are on her side, touching down
and lifting off before her feet can grow
steady on the ground. And just as surely
as her rhythm is a cycle, the cycle
a wave, the wave a song with no
purpose but to sing itself, she steps
in time with the dervishing planets,
the snoring tides, the faucets leaking

all over creation. I used to see
the eye as a prism, projecting the future
on its upside-down screen, but now
I see it as the narrows of an hourglass,
itself a victim of time, the future above,
all past below, converging and retreating
from this moment that divides or at least
separates the two. The rope skips
like a broken metaphor whose meaning
degrades in the noise of settling sand
as even my own double-helical signal
will decay, grow indistinguishable
in time, an arc of ciphers spliced
in the length of a patchwork spiral.
Already I have reached the point
where all that I remember exceeds
all that I can expect—but does my eye
divide or merely separate what's been
from what will be? Is this moment
like a bead on a hoop, a planet
on an orbit, keeping the same arc,
though moving, before and after?
And this stranger, this wonder
skipping rope, unwittingly pacing
my heart that can't go on like this

forever—her eye will see only
the last half of my life, as I
will see the first of hers:
Between the two, do we make a whole,
or do we simply join our arcs
to the longer spiral, a succession of lines
like the frames of a film reel,
or the rungs of a ladder
whose both ends fade into a darkness
receding and pursuing as we go?

# Without a Sequel

Everywhere he looked he said goodbye.
Every word he spoke was large with parting,
parting getting harder as he got better at it.
He saw the face of days begin to flake
like weathered homes and home grow cold
with hollow rooms. He mouthed the names
until his throat grew choked with slurry silt,
held photos in his palm they curled like fish.
He rubbed the burlap of his skin his muscles
creaked like rope his blood was wood.
He listened to his heart his heart was slowing.
He willed his arms be warm a little longer,
hooped them round the world the world slipped through.
He wrapped them round his head his ears were singing.
He couldn't free the glacier of his tongue.
He wept the dew that grows on stone
and slowed to stone, his lungs a fossil bed,
his tendons tar, his song a bone.
Everywhere he looked his loss called stay.
Everything he turned to turned away.